Many people who struggle with compulsive behaviors such as drinking, smoking, gambling and overeating want to stop, but they can't. Brian Mulipah is the recovery coach who has created a framework that helps them to stop their addictions and prevent relapse long term, so they can start living the life they've always wanted, without the constant threat of relapse.

If your relapse or compulsive behaviors have significantly negatively affected your relationships and you could do with help, email Brian on BrianMulipah@gmail.com

Important

Many people who struggle with compulsive behaviors including, but not limited to: drinking, smoking, gambling shopping and overeating want to stop their addictions, but they can't, they struggle with relapse. This prompt and writing notebook is designed as a strategy for you to work your recovery through processing your emotions, writing short stories about life, yourself or simply taking notes whenever and wherever you are. You may use this as your recovery journal and diary where you can write out and or draw life as you experience it.

If you are in rehab, you can use this place to journal your personal recovery as you experience the program. If you have completed rehab or you attend any support groups, you may take advantage and journal your recovery and experiences through the use of the prompt questions?

This relapse prevention and addiction recovery prompt journal was designed with the support of Brian Mulipah a recovery coach who helps others to stop their addictions and prevent relapse long term. For recovery coaching and support, you can contact Brian on BrianMulipah@gmail.com

As a valued friend in recovery, we want to provide you with the best recovery experience possible. By contributing a product review of this book on any online retailer, you'll assist others in making more informed decisions while also helping us to provide better service for yourself and new fellow friends in recovery in the future. Would you please, at some point, take a moment and share your perspectives?

What will really make the biggest difference in your life?

What does a great week look like for you?

If you woke up with courage, how could your life change?

What's the worst that can happen this year, and can you handle that?

How would your life be transformed if you changed this right now?

Why does your personal development matter?

How can you create more value with less effort?

What are some steps that you can take this week towards achieving your best life?

Who do you need to become in order to succeed?

Who might get hurt if you don't get better?

What did you accomplish this week?

What do you need most right now?

Have you thought about the impact you'll have by creating a new life?

How are you taking care of yourself?

How can you enjoy the process of your personal growth?

How have you changed the world for generations to come?

What needs your immediate attention?

What goal are you ready to achieve?

How have you grown this week?

Are you approaching your life from your head or from your heart?

Are you living in your power or pleasing someone else?

What rules do you have that are getting in your way?

What did you learn this week?

What are you wasting your time with?

How will you transform your life this week?

Which step could you take that would make the biggest difference, right now?

What can you do today to get you on track to your best life?

Who might benefit from your failure?

What keeps tripping you up?

Have you solved any problems this week?

What gets you out of bed each day?

How can you use your past to your advantage?

What holds you back physically, psychologically, socially and spiritually?

What gifts aren't being fully developed?

Are you in recovery or wishing for it?

What are you looking for in using this book?

Whose life are you living?

What could you be happy about if you chose to be?

What opportunities are you missing?

What's the biggest challenge you have?

What's your strategy to achieve your goals?

What does your ideal life look like?

What assumptions are you making?

What are you grateful for?

Is there a single change worth making?

On a scale of 1 – 10 how honest have you been to your family?

How will you test your ideas?

In what way is your best life in alignment with your values?

Would your personal development help you earn more?

Who is taking advantage of you?

What are you willing to stop doing to improve your situation?

What's the downside of your dream?

What is your most important project?

How perfect is your life?

Is the use of this book giving you energy or draining your energy?

Do you have a detailed strategy to achieve your goals?

What's possible for you financially?

What will your legacy be?

Are you focused on what's wrong or what's right?

If you weren't scared, what would you do?

How can you get your needs fully met?

If your biggest weakness were also your biggest strength, what would that be like?

Who's grateful for you?

What is currently motivating you?

What does your intuition tell you about your recovery?

What could keep you from getting the life you want?

What skill do you most want to learn?

What's next for you?

How could a 12 step sponsor, addiction counselor or recovery coach assist you?

What measurable results are important in your life?

What's your strategy for becoming a better individual?

Are you acting on faith or fear?

On a scale of 1 to 10, how ready for the next level of your life?

What will your impact be 100 years from now?

If your life were exclusively oriented around your values, what would that be like?

Who wouldn't like it if you succeeded?

What's stopping you this week?

How will you know if you are going in the right (or wrong) direction?

What might make the difference that could change everything?

On a scale of 1 – 10 how honest have you been to yourself?

What are you pretending not to know?

What are you grateful for this week?

If you don't change this, what will it cost you in the long run?

If you could have anything, what would you have right now?

How can you improve your life, so it adds value forever?

Are your personal standards high enough to reach your goals?

How would you describe the difference between a need and a value?

How will you know if you are overextending yourself?

Where are you falling behind?

Who did you serve this week?

What's holding you back the most?

What are you willing to commit to improve your life?

What needs to happen to change your life?

Are your goals pulling you forward or are you struggling to reach them?

Which of your core values can you think of today?

What plan do you need in order to achieve your new goals?

What's the dream you've given up on?

Does your current environment fully support who you're becoming?

What are you waiting for?

What's the first step you need to take to reach your goal?

Who can help you with getting better?

What's great about your life this week?

What changes should you make now?

How might you get help from others?

Are you using your past to grow or are you using it to beat yourself up?

Is there anything you need to start delegating?

Have you decided to take action or are you just hoping you will?

What will you have to give up in order to make room for your goals?

What is your most urgent problem?

What's standing in your way?

What does your inner wisdom say about your best life?

Where do you want to be in 5 years?

Who are you responsible for?

What interests you most about your personal recovery and recovery?

What are you putting up with?

What is the meaning of your life?

Who else will benefit from your recovery or personal wellness?

What's stopping you from taking action?

Many people who struggle with compulsive behaviors such as drinking, smoking, gambling and overeating want to stop, but they can't. Brian Mulipah is the recovery coach who has created a framework that helps them to stop their addictions and prevent relapse long term, so they can start living the life they've always wanted.

If your relapse or compulsive behaviors have significantly negatively affected your relationships and you could do with help, email Brian on BrianMulipah@gmail.com

Made in the USA
Columbia, SC
12 January 2022

54182625R00070